ALL THE POEMS

MURIEL SPARK was born in Edinburgh in 1918. After some years living in Africa, she returned to England, where she edited *Poetry Review* from 1947 to 1949 and published her first volume of poems, *The Fanfarlo*, in 1952. She eventually made her home in Italy. Her many novels include *Memento Mori* (1959), *The Prime of Miss Jean Brodie* (1961), *The Girls of Slender Means* (1963), *The Abbess of Crewe* (1974), *A Far Cry from Kensington* (1988) and *The Finishing School* (2004). Her short stories were collected in 1967, 1985 and 2001; her *Collected Poems* appeared in 1967. Dame Muriel was made Commandeur des Arts et des Lettres (France) in 1996 and awarded her DBE in 1993.

D1494403

MURIEL SPARK

All the Poems

CARCANET

ACKNOWLEDGEMENTS

Grateful acknowledgements are made to the editors and publishers of the magazines and newspapers in which these poems first appeared.

The following poems first appeared in *The New Yorker*: 'Conversation Piece', 'The Dark Music of the Rue du Cherche-Midi', 'Edinburgh Villanelle', 'The Messengers', 'Canaan', 'The Card Party', 'Created and Abandoned', 'The Empty Space', 'Holidays', 'Mungo Bays the Moon', 'That Bad Cold' and 'That Lonely Shoe Lying on the Road'.

Others appeared in *The Times Literary Supplement*, *The New York Times Sophisticated Traveler*, *Penguin New Writing No. 15*, *Poetry Quarterly*, *Scotland on Sunday*, *The Scotsman*, *The Tatler* and *World Literature Today*.

First published in Great Britain in 2004 by
Carcanet Press Limited
Alliance House
Cross Street
Manchester M2 7AQ

This paperback edition first published 2006

First published in the United States in 2004 by New Directions Books
80 Eighth Avenue
New York 10011

Original book design by Sylvia Frezzolini Severance

A CIP catalogue record for this book is available from the British Library
ISBN 1 85754 890 6
978 1 85754 890 7

The publisher acknowledges financial assistance from Arts Council England

Printed and bound in England by SRP Ltd, Exeter

CONTENTS

From the Latin

FOREWORD

The poems in this book were composed throughout my literary life, from the late 1940s to the present day.

My editor, Barbara Epler (who, for wisdom, charm, humour and intuition, must be the envy of every author), has here re-arranged my poems in an order which, I think, gives more coherence and novelty to a work than would a chronological arrangement. I feel that my poems, like some of my memories, come together in a manner entirely involuntary and unforseen.

As far as chronology is concerned, I have no exact records and dates. In my early days I often had to wait years for the eventual publication of a piece of creative work. Some of these poems were written from the late-forties onward, although not published until later. In the list of contents I have tried to indicate by the useful "*c.*" the year to which I think the poems belong.

Once, when I went to visit a beloved friend, the poet W. H. Auden, I found him "touching up" his earlier poetry. He told me that he had been unfavourably criticized for this habit, but he felt justified in making the changes because he understood, now in his mature years, what he had really meant but failed to express precisely, when he was young.

I thought of this when I looked through my poems. In some cases I was not even sure what I meant at the time. Fifty years ago, in some senses, I was a different person. And yet, I can't disapprove of those poems whose significance and origins I forget. *Edinburgh Villanelle* for instance: what did I mean by "Heart of Midlothian, never mine."? There is a spot outside St. Giles Cathedral in Edinburgh, my native city, which marks the "Heart of Midlothian." I have fond memories of Edinburgh. My pivotal book, *The Prime of Miss Jean Brodie*, was a novel about Edinburgh. I have no idea what I meant by the words in the poem, "never mine", and yet I meant them at the time. And I have let them rest as they are, along with other unfathomable lines.

Although most of my life has been devoted to fiction, I have always thought of myself as a poet. I do not write 'poetic' prose, but feel that my outlook on life and my perceptions of events are those of a poet. Whether in prose or verse, all creative writing is mysteriously connected with music and I always hope this factor is apparent throughout my work.

Long ago, I studied verse-forms in detail, and attempted to practise them. Not all were in my view successful enough to be offered in the present volume. But I can state my conviction that, for creative writing of any sort, an early apprenticeship as a poet is a wonderful stimulant and start.

MURIEL SPARK
TUSCANY, 2003

ALL THE POEMS OF
Muriel Spark

A Tour of London

I. DAYBREAK COMPOSITION

Anyone in this top-floor flat
This morning, might look out upon
An oblong canvas of Kensington
Almost ready for looking at.

Houses lean sideways to the light;
At foreground left, a crowd of trees
Is blue, is a footman, his gloves are white.
The sky's a pair of legs, top-right,
The colour of threadbare dungarees.

All the discrepant churches grind
Four, and in the window frame is
Picasso at least, his scene; its name is
Morning; authentic, but never signed.

II. KENSINGTON GARDENS

Old ladies and tulips, model boats,
Compact babies, mobile mothers,
Distant buses like parakeets,
Lonely men with mackintoshes

Over their arms—where do they go?
Where come from? now that summer's
Paraphernalia and splash is
Out, as if planted a year ago.

1

III. WHAT THE STRANGER WONDERED

Where does she come from
Sipping coffee alone in London?

The shoes, the hair—I do not think
She has anything in the bank.

Has she a man, where is he then,
Why is she sitting at half-past ten

Reading a book alone in London?
Where does the money come from

That lets her be alone and sipping
Not with a man, not in a job, not with a dog
   to the grocer tripping?

IV. DAY OF REST

The clock knocked off at quarter to three
And sat there yawning with arms stretched wide,
And it was set going again by nobody,
It being Sunday and we being occupied.

Therefore the day happened and disappeared,
But whether the time we kept was appropriate
To rend, to sew, to love, to hate,
No one could say for certain; all that occurred
Was Sunday, London, bells, talk, fate.

V. SUBURB

It is the market clock that moonish glows.
Where two hands point, two poplars interlock.
Night's verities knock
Normal perspectives comatose,
Proving the moon a market clock,
The trees, time's laughing-stock.

VI. THE HOUSE

Their last look round was happening when
The bus pulled up outside.
Nothing burning? Windows tried?
The lights go on and off again
And they are satisfied,
And we already starting off—
But see the house, how curious,
The lights again! and sure enough,
Feeling the catch behind the curtain
A hand—just to make certain.

VII. MAN IN THE STREET

Last thing at night and only one
Man in the street,
And even he was gone complete
Into an absence as he stood
Beside the lamplight longitude.
He stood so long and still, it would
Take men in longer streets to find
What this was chewing in his mind.

The Dark Music of the Rue du Cherche-Midi

If you should ask me, is there a street of Europe,
and where, and what, is that ultimate street?
I would answer: the one-time Roman road
in Paris, on the left bank of the river,
the long, long Rue du Cherche-Midi,
street of my thoughts and afterthoughts
and curiosity never to be satisfied entirely, and
premonitions, inconceivably shaped, and memories.

Suppose that I looked for the street of my life, where I always
could find an analogy. There in the
shop-front windows and in the courtyards,
the alleys, the great doorways, old convents, baronial properties:
those of the past. And new
hotels of the present, junk shops, bead shops,
pastry cooks, subtle chocolate-makers, florists of intricate
wonder, and merchants of exceptional fabrics.
Suppose that I looked, I would choose to
find that long, long Rue, of Paris, du Cherche-Midi, its buildings,
they say, so tall they block out the
sun. I have always thought it worth
the chase and the search to find some sort of meridian.

From 1662 to the Revolution:
No. 7, owned in 1661 by
Jérémie Derval, financier, counsellor,
and master of the king's household.

All along the street:
Marquises, dukes, duchesses,
financiers, mathematicians, magistrates,

philosophers, bibliophiles, prioresses,
abbesses, princes and, after them,
their widows, generals, ambassadors,
politicians. Some
were beheaded and others took over. In essence
none has departed. No. 38:
there was the military prison where Dreyfus
first stood trial, in December, 1894.
At No. 40 resided the Comte de Rochambeau until
he was sent to help George Washington;
he forced the English to surrender at Yorktown and took
twenty-two flags from them. What a street, the Rue du Cherche-Midi!

Here, Nos. 23–31, was a convent where a famous abbess reigned,
disgusted in girlhood by her father, a lecher,
she imposed a puritan rule and was admired,
especially when, great lady that she was,
she humbled herself to wash the dishes.

Beads and jewels of long ago look out
from their dark shopwindows
like blackberries in a wayside bramble bush
holding out their arms:
Take me, pick me, I am dark and sweet,
ripe and moist with life.
The haggard young girl in charge of the boutique
reaches for the beads, she fondles them, sad, sad,
to part with such a small but
undeniable treasure. Rose quartz:
she sells it with eager reluctance.
Listen to my music. Hear it.
Raindrops, each dark note.
She has not slept well. Her little
black dress was hastily donned, and the half-
circles are drooping under her eyes.

They say the Rue du Cherche-Midi,
with its tall houses set at shadowy angles,
never catches the sun.

Still, in the shop, that
raddled, dignified young girl—
frugal, stylish,
experienced—will, with bony fingers,
pick out a pile of necklaces:
the very one that you want, those
opals, those moonstones.

Dark boutiques, concerns; their shadow falls
over the bright appointments of the day.
It is a long, long past that haunts the street of Europe,
a spirit of vast endurance,
a certain music, Rue du Cherche-Midi.

They did not intend to distinguish between the essence
Of wit and wallpaper trellis. What they cared
Was how the appointments of the age appeared
Under the citron gaslight incandescence.

Virtue was vulgar, sin a floral passion
And death a hansom at the door, while they
Kept faith with a pomaded sense of history
In their fashion.

Behind the domino, those fringed and fanned
Exclusive girls, prinked with the peacock's eye
Noted, they believed, the trickle of a century
Like a thin umbrella in a black-gloved hand.

A black velvet embroidered handbag full of medium-size carrots
All of which said 'Good morning' in one voice.
What does the dream mean?

The black velvet is death; and the embroidery?
Oh, I daresay, a fancy funeral.
The carrots are sex, plenty of them.

Why did they say 'Good morning'?

Well, I said 'Good morning' back to them,
This in my dream being the right thing to do.

Verlaine Villanelle

Like poor Verlaine, whom God defend,
I see the sky above the roof,
And write my book till summer's end.

When tree, town, bell and birdnote blend,
I feel, since summer sails aloof
Like poor Verlaine, whom God defend,

Who went to jail but did not mend.
I taste the pity sure enough
And write my book till summer's end.

I see a tree, and won't pretend
I'm warped on that nostalgic woof
Like poor Verlaine, whom God defend.

But rue the crooked dividend
These days will yield of galley-proof,
And write my book till summer's end.

Therefore I see the sky and spend
An hour of lyrical reproof,
Like poor Verlaine, whom God defend,
And write my book till summer's end.

Edinburgh Villanelle

These eyes that saw the saturnine
Glance in my back, refused the null
Heart of Midlothian, never mine.

Hostile High Street gave the sign.
Hollyrood made unmerciful
These eyes that saw the saturnine

Watchmen of murky Leith begin
To pump amiss the never-full
Heart of Midlothian, never mine.

Withal they left the North Sea brine
Seeping the slums and did not fool
These eyes that saw the saturnine

Waters no provident whim made wine
Fail to infuriate the dull
Heart of Midlothian, never mine.

Municipal monuments confine
What ghosts return to ridicule
These eyes that saw the saturnine
Heart of Midlothian, never mine.

Holy Water Rondel

For salt, no word seems apposite;
Its common wisdom would defy
All praise, so far as meets the eye,
Salt is so meek a hypocrite.

And not the most selective wit
Has words to measure water by,
Because, so far as meets the eye,
Water is exquisite.

But cited sacerdotally,
Multiple evils up and quit,
Which proves that water and salt commit
Pathetic faults beyond the eye;

And shows a happy flaw whereby
The fabric is bereft of it,
Since there is nothing left of it
But mercies more than meet the eye.

Therefore I rate the creatures high
Whose salt and watery features knit
So strict and strange a composite
Of blessings and of brine thereby.

No wonder that the clergy ply
The people every week with it,
Who are of virtue infinite
So far as meets the eye.

'There is,' he declared.

'Really?' she grinned.

'Undoubtedly,' he stated.

'Tomorrow,' she burbled.

'A majority,' he chortled.

' The statues?' she enquired.

'Public health,' he opined.

'The signature,' she ventured.

'Miss Universe,' he emoted.

'The confederation,' she growled.

'Hostile ethics!' he exclaimed.

'The Tears of Time,' she choked.

'Everything entire,' he warbled.

'It's a mere obsession,' she roared.

'Develop the wolf,' he demanded.

'Done,' she snarled.

'On with the job,' he guffawed.

'Not unanimous,' she yelled.

'You're breaking my jaw,' he groaned.

'Silence!' she sneered.

Authors' Ghosts

I think that authors' ghosts creep back
Nightly to haunt the sleeping shelves
And find the books they wrote.
Those authors put final, semi-final touches,
Sometimes whole paragraphs.

Whole pages are added, re-written, revised,
So deeply by night those authors employ
Themselves with those old books of theirs.

How otherwise
Explain the fact that maybe after years
Have passed, the reader
Picks up the book—But was it like that?
I don't remember this . . . Where
Did this ending come from?
I recall quite another.

Oh yes, it has been tampered with
No doubt about it—
The author's very touch is here, there and there,
Where it wasn't before, and
What's more, something's missing—
I could have sworn . . .

That Bad Cold

That hand, a tiny one, first at my throat;
That thump in the chest.
I know you of old, you're a bad cold
Come to stay for a few days,
Unwanted visitor—a week perhaps.

Nobody asked him to come. (Yes,
He is masculine, but otherwise
Don't try to parse the situation.)
Everything stops. Perhaps
He is providentially intended to
Make cease and desist an overworking
State of mind. Yes, there is a certain
Respite. Friends mean merely a bed
And a hot drink. Enemies and all
Paranoias, however justified, lose their way
In the fog. And the desk diary
Lies open with a vacant grin.

Leaning Over an Old Wall

Leaning over an old wall, gazing
into a dark pool, waiting like a moonling to see
only the water traffic, fish and frogs
I saw my image stare at me, appraising.

Suddenly a voice spoke from a stone
in the bed of the pool, saying
it is the pebble on the path you tread,
it is the tomb's substance,
it pillows your head,
it is the cold heart lamenting alone,
it is all these things, the stone said.

A willow moaned, it is your despair,
it is your unrest and your grieving,
your fears that have been and those that are to be,
it is your unbelieving
and the wanhope of your days, said the tree.

And the roots of the willow, lying
under the bed of the pool were crying,
it is the twisted cord that feeds this tree
which is your clay and entity;
it is the filament that fed your birth;
from your wanton seed
into the faithful earth
impulsive tendons lead.

But the green reeds sang, it is the voice
of your life's joy.
It is the green word that springs

amazing from your frost, it flings
arms to the sky so that the clouds rejoice
and the sun sings.

Flower Into Animal

This is the pain that sea anemones bear
in the fear of aberration but wilfully
aspiring to respire in another
more difficult way, and turning
flower into animal interminably.

It is a pain to choke with, when the best
of a species gets lost somewhere.
Different, indifferent pain—
to be never the one again to act like the rest
but answer to the least of another kind;
to be here no more to savour nor desist,

but to identify maybe the grains of sand
and call anonymous grasses by their name,
to find remembrance if the streets run seabound;
when the tide enters the room, when the roof gives flower
cry Credo to the obdurate weed.

And to have to put up with the pain and process,
nor look back to delight the eyes
that ache with the displacement of all sights.
And to have to alter the trunk of a tree to a dragon
if it should be required, or the river to a swan.

Abroad

Abroad is peculiar names above the shops.
Strange, too, the cookery and the cops. The people
Prattle with tongues there, they rattle
Inscrutable money, and with foreign eyes
Follow your foreign eccentricities.

Going up to Sotheby's

This was the wine. It stained the top of the page
when she knocked over the glass accidentally. A pity, she said,
to lose that drop. For the wine was a treat.
Here's a coffee-cup ring, and another. He preferred coffee to tea.
Some pages re-written entirely, scored through, cancelled over
and over
on this, his most important manuscript.

That winter they took a croft in Perthshire,
living on oats and rabbits bought for a few pence from
the madman.
The children thrived, and she got them to school daily,
mostly by trudge.
He was glad to get the children out of the way, but always
felt cold
while working on his book. This
is his most important manuscript, completed 1929.
'Children, go and play outside. Your father's trying to work.
But keep away from the madman's house.'
He looked up from his book. 'There's nothing
wrong with the madman.' Which was true.

She typed out the chapters in the afternoons. He looked
happily at her.
He worked best late at night.
'Aren't you ever coming to bed? I often wonder,
are you married to me or to your bloody book?'
A smudge on the page, still sticky after all these years.
Something greasy on the last page.
This is that manuscript, finished in the late spring,
crossed-out, dog-eared; this, the original,

passed through several literary hands while
the pages she had typed were at the publishers'.
One personage has marked a passage with red ink,
has written in the margin, 'Are you *sure?*'

Five publishers rejected it in spite of recommendations.
The sixth decided to risk his pounds sterling down the drain
for the sake of prestige. The author was a difficult customer.
                                                    However,
they got the book published at last.
Her parents looked after the children while the couple went
                                                    to France
for a short trip. This bundle of paper, the original manuscript,
went into a fibre trunk, got damp into it, got mouldy and furled.
It took fifteen more years for him to make his reputation,
by which time the children had grown up, Agnes as a
secretary at the BBC, Leo as a teacher.

The author died in '48, his wife in '68.
Agnes and Leo married and begat.

And now the grandchildren are selling the manuscript.
Bound and proud, documented and glossed
by scholars of the land, smoothed out
and precious, these leaves of paper
are going up to Sotheby's. The wine-stained,
stew-stained and mould-smelly papers are
going up to Sotheby's. They occupy the front seat
of the Renault, beside the driver.
They are a national event. They are going up
to make their fortune at last,
which once were so humble, tattered, and so truly working class.

On the Lack of Sleep

Lying on the roof of everything I listen
To the breath of ambition in her sleep, to the gasp of rancour
Turning in her dream. And the parting of lovers, the
                                      coming together
Of old divisions, the meeting and retreating of   partners
       Cease, though I do not sleep.

Already I have wandered through fields of Michaelmas
                           flowers. Tired
As I am, I remember the counting of all souls, think of their
                                blue faces
I sought so long and discovered at last in the house below,
       Asleep, though I do not cease,

Though I persist into the day without motive as in the first hour
Of my life, tired as I am, I see the innocence I am left with.
Honour yawns, vanity foams in her coma, charity stretches
       A sham, luxurious limb.
Until I gather you again when I come into my own,
       Lie low, my sleepy fortunes.

This is the grave that time dug.
This is the box
  that lay in the grave that time dug.
This is the hand
  that rapped on the box
    that lay in the grave that time dug.
This is the stove
  that warmed the hand
    that rapped on the box
      that lay in the grave that time dug.

This is the child an instant born
  that lit the stove
    that warmed the hand
      that rapped on the box
        that lay in the grave that time dug.
This is the pink deceptive thorn
  that bled the child an instant born
    that lit the stove
      that warmed the hand
        that rapped on the box
          that lay in the grave that time dug.

This is the alderman bound and sworn
  that planted the pink deceptive thorn
    that bled the child an instant born
      that lit the stove
        that warmed the hand
          that rapped on the box
            that lay in the grave that time dug.

The Pearl-Miners

By night I watch a fitful tribe
Along the street advance and halt.
Time and again their limbs describe
A proud protracted somersault.

Blank-eyed beneath the lamp they steer
Compliant hips with hands of chalk.
I know them by their grief, and hear
Convulsions tolling in their talk.

They come, contemptuous and fleet
In tartan jeans, in ochre tights,
To make overt their counterfeit
Drowsy exotic appetites.

They are asleep and cannot rest,
Dismayed in far delirium.
Elaborately they attest
The dreaded labours still to come.

I know them by the lights of fear
On their elliptic faces falling.
This way and that, they haul the gear
And apparatus of their calling.

So obsolete, the block they drag,
So bitterly they drill and grind,
So deep beneath the pavement flag
They dig for pearls and do not find.

So freakish, they descend and storm
The black foundations, and in vain
They rise distracted to perform
Their supplicating rites again.

High-style they flash, akimbo fall,
Entreating on their shaken heads
That pale magnetic mineral
Which lugged them from their sundry beds.

Full-wheel the rounds revolve alike:
The sleepers turn, and cheek by cheek,
Dig up the road and do not strike
The lustrous milky seam they seek.

I recognise them by their fear;
So fair the dream, so far the sight.
The lambent virtues are not here
In Kensington of dreadful night.

You boys of amber, quit your load;
You emerald, you marble girls,
Not underneath Old Brompton Road
Nestle the subterranean pearls.

I know these miners comfortless,
And by their pain identify
Pearl within pearl, since I possess
None but my bane to measure by,

None but their sleep to waken me,
None but their sorrow to confide
What pleasures have forsaken me,
None but my foe to be my guide.

I reckon only by their lack,
Rich within perfection furled,
And, by the sepulchre they hack,
Perceive the living underworld.

Here they have come, my fake, my lost,
My own familiars to their grave.
By vicious lights like elm-trees tossed,
Their bright pathetic branches wave.

So high the fault, the dream so true;
So low, the lovely mind persists
Immaculate, but not for you,
Dissevered, sad somnambulists.

Here is the time of watching birds;
senses mingle and show their hands.
Now is the place where the signal stands

that points an omen from both my doors;
though the street shall talk like a hammer,
walls keep silence over my shoulder.

The wrong key in the right door
ponders the portent. Which window
saw where I have been to-morrow?

where I rocked my house on the water;
doors moved like an ark turning
back her face, and this is a meaning.

For the unlucky eye never shall taste
the bright bow of my vision again,
but this error, bitter as brine,

shall blind the eyes that heard the day
before my fairweather foes came,
those that crossed my fingers dumb.

Fault, fault, on both my houses—
Speed, bonny ark, and change your shape
until the ominous birds fly up.

My Kingdom for a Horse

Having considered the place, having decided
There was not room enough, nevertheless
As nine o'clock shivered the dark balcony
I heard horses beating by;
And saw, below, white-coated riders, white-sided
Beasts blanketed against the cold and skyless
And groundless general benightment.
It was a white presentment
With one red light before, one red behind it.

'They pass every night.' Because
Of this I came to stay, small as it was.
Smaller still by daylight; much crockery
Had to go; many books were abandoned; so too,
A hoard of smooth planks, they had to go.

It is not altogether a mockery.
Horses alone I could not greatly care for,
But this by night is a company so corporate,
I call it a Horse, of regimental state.
Let no prodigal neighbour spend me therefore:
I am aware of this obvious school of riding,
And do not count it remarkable that late
And locally flies the Horse. What's to be wondered at
Is myself, that nightly to be dundered at
From a street without moment the whole length of it,
I mark the nine o'clock Horse, residing
Here, hemmed-in, on the strength of it.

The old ridiculous partner is back again
who speaks my mind before me, singing me now
fonder than ever, my embarrassing vancourier.

I am her fool, the noisy one to follow
years at a time, and know her for my other
who sounds my superstition like a bagpipe.

I am her acrobat and altogether
lacking an answer loud enough I
somersault to her tune, how sick soever.

I left her once
for seven years long:
then she piped
and I did not dance.

Little it recks that
seven long years
I wept not
although she mourned,

since she is back again and the mood is on.

So must I bear my old she-wolf, who once
suckled the rising moon,
to blow her pipes, and I will dance again.

I'm sorry I can't come to-day;
I have dozens of letters
   to write.

   Oh, letters. You and your
     dozens of letters.

Yes, I've let them pile up
   by the gross
And to-day's the day of
   reckoning.

   Oh, leave your letters, just
     let them lie.

       •

I'm sorry I can't come to-day;
I have received a letter.

   A letter!

Yes, a letter. I have to
   attend to it to-day.

   Of course, of course, let's
     make it another day.

The month of the holidays,
where is the . . . who can find
him . . . the electrician, there
is a water problem, the oil tank
leaks, do you know what
that means? It is the holidays, there are
no electricians, no shops, no tanks,
no cisterns. Nails
are breaking, blood does not gush.
Ring, ring, ring, dial 023
dial 576 and 999. Nothing
doing, my friend. All the machines
are dead. Money doesn't speak.
Nobody. The desert.

    And now come the floods.
Escape, escape quickly. Leave
everything. No point in locking
up.

    Go away, far far away. The
month of the holidays.

Facts

Father was a debt-collector
Mother *casalinga* (Italian for housewife)
Siamese cat
favourite son
and an outcast son.

Go off on a holiday.
Leave the outcast at home.

What holiday? Drugs? Marocco? Where?
Never seen again.

Cleaned up the camper like new & sold it.

He had a place in London

Took 9 mil. lire (about three thousand pounds)
                    out of the bank.
DNA blood; tiny bit.

Yes, shot them all—pointed out graves,
can't find bodies.

What happened to the cat?

Complaint in a Wash-out Season

My mind's in pickle. Think of my talents all soused
in rainwater, April you All Fools' Month, you've doused
the light of your joke. Call off this protracted
intransigent deluge, it's hackneyed;
nothing to grizzle about now—winter's gone knock-kneed,
so turn off the tap,
you monstrous infant wetting Infinity's lap.
You turned the garden hose on;
you spat a million missiles aslant through a hundred dozen
long-range peashooters. You should be past
practical jokes in bad taste;
and what an old has-been you look when you flash
in the face of the sun in a shot-silk taffeta sash
and lift the petticoat clouds and dance a fandango.
You've rinsed the guaranteed colours out of the rainbow.
At least, when you wash your dye-streaked hair,
be so kind as to shake it out elsewhere,
and request the adenoidal firmament
not to sneeze all over my temperament.

Litany of Time Past

What's today?
  Hoops today.
What's yesterday?
  Tops yesterday.
What's tomorrow?
  Diabolo.

Moons and planets come out to play,
The Bear bowled, the Sun spun.
See the Devil-on-sticks run
Today, tomorrow, and yesterday.

What's Hope?
  Skipping rope.
What's Charity?
  Salty peppery.
What's Faith?
  Edinburgh, Leith,
  Portobello, Musselburgh,
  and Dalkeith.

Out you are.
  In you are.
Mustard.
  Vinegar.

The European Bison fell from grace.
So did the white-tailed Gnu.
Likewise the Blesbok, as also the Mountain Zebra.
The Giant Tortoise must have sinned too.

Everyone knows about the Dodo;
The same goes for the Great Auk.
The inoffensive Okapi's crime
Was trying to be other beasts at the same time.
And there is the case of the Blue-Buck.

They all came to a halt and are dissolved in mystery.
Who remembers, now, Steller's cullionly Sea-Cow?
It, too, through its innocent fault
Failed the finals in history.

Faith and Works

My friend is always doing Good
But doubts the Meaning of his labour,
While I by Faith am much imbued
And can't be bothered with my Neighbour.

These mortal heresies in us
Friendship makes orthodox and thus
We are the truest Saints alive
As near as two and two make five.

Conundrum

As I was going to Handover Fists
I met a man with seven wrists.
The seven wrists had seven hands;
The seven hands bore seven bonds;
The seven bonds hid seven wounds:
How many were going to Handover Fists?

And as I was going to Kingdom Come
I met a dog of twenty ton.
The twenty ton had twenty parts;
The twenty parts bore twenty hearts;
The twenty hearts gave twenty barks:
How many were going to Kingdom Come?

The Messengers

Arriving late sometimes and never
Quite expected, still they come,
Bringing a folded meaning home
Between the lines, inside the letter.

As a scarecrow in the harvest
Turns an innocent field to grief
These tattered hints are dumb and deaf,
But bring the matter to a crisis.

They are the messengers who run
Onstage to us who try to doubt them,
Fetching our fate to hand; without them
What would Sophocles have done?

Mr. Chiddicott, being a bachelor,
Purchased from a reputable department store
(Barkers') a morning-tea machine
At the price of fifteen pounds fifteen.
Easy to work, all plugged and wired.
Each night, he set the time required,
And every morning when he heard
The bell, he found his tea prepared.
But being by profession something mechanic
Mr. Chiddicott began to perfect it,
So that before long when it woke him up
It actually handed him the cup.

Years pass. Mr. Chiddicott grows
Successful as a cabbage rose,
Mellow, unmated and serene,
Served by the morning-tea machine.
Alas, the transience of bliss—
There came a sudden end to his.

One morning as it rang the bell,
The tea-machine said, 'What the hell,
I've stood this treatment long and dumb;
Mr. Chiddicott, the time has come
For you to make the tea instead.
Nip out and let me into bed.'
And when our friend demurred, alack,
The tea-machine gave him a dreadful crack.
Mr. Chiddicott murmured as he curled
Up, 'It is the end of the world.'

But it wasn't, for Mr. Chiddicott came
To, and finally admitted blame,
And every morning now he can be seen
(From the windows across the street, I mean)
Serving tea to his perfected tea-machine.

To you, fretful exemplar, who claim to place
Love before all success and kindness above
Any career, I answer yes, well said, my dear,
If you have the particular choice:
If you're gifted, I mean, in love
And also special in life's performances.
But are you so very clever and so very nice?

Mungo Bays the Moon

My dog Mungo under my window
Barks in the dark. Is that an owl?
What fowl? What foe? His note ends
                in a howl
So now I know. He bays the
full-bellied moon, my Mungo dog.

Here in Tuscany they say
Never move the wine when the moon
                is full,
Never prune the trees while she waxes.
Your hair your nails your beard are
                growing long
With the swelling moon, the moon, and
                Mungo's song
Declares the same. Magnetic moon
He howls, my Mungo dog. Pregnant
                ball in the sky,
Most pregnant, listen-to-me, my serenade,
                my howl.

He comes out of his kennel to sing
                in the night,
My Mungo, my brown dog.

Scream scream I am
being victimized wickedized
You are he said to me
a destroyer
an enemy
and I will dish he said
the dirt scream scream
You can't do this to me I wish
you dead my job my life
hand over your purse
he said immediately or I
scream scream and worse I
am a scholar I spook I rake
I lose my voice
every dollar counts I'll do worse
scream scream I am.

The Hospital

I want to fall asleep in the chair
                    by the bed.
Someone calls from the corridor:
Tom! I must keep her records up
                    deck o'cards
                    neck of duck
(That's up to them) I myself
want to fall asleep on fine sheets,
                    don't you think?
Who will keep my eyes shut?

The Empty Space

A square space on the wall
marks the memory of that picture
painted at night, stolen at night,
worked on at night, in Rome, from the
                              artist's window.
How I remember Castel St. Angelo
in her night picture, gleaming with
history-in-darkness, guardian of old Rome,
and the artist's home was full of midnight
and the light of all Europe shone in her hands.
She painted till dawn, having thought
to herself one night, I will paint
that scene, and started
and patiently full-heartedly pursued it
and did it completely—large, dark and light.
My honest close companion on the wall:
It is all over now. The thieves came by night.

I was writing a poem called
    Hats.

I had seen a shop window
    in Venice, full of
      Hats.

There were hats for morning,
    for evening, men's hats, girls'
      Hats.

There were hats for fishing
And hats dating back to
    Death in Venice
His hat so Panama, hers such a
    Madame de Staël
      Hat.

I was writing a poem about
    Hats
Hats for a garden party, hats
For a wet day, hats for a
    wedding party, a
    memorial service.

There were hats for golf and
Hats for tennis. Bowler hats,
Top hats for the races, floral
    headgears equally.

And as I wrote this poem
Sitting in a square with my coffee,
I was called over to see a friend.
Only for an instant. I shoved
The poem in my handbag and
I slung the bag over the chair.

Only an instant.
And gone, gone forever, handbag
    poem, my hats, my hats.

Also my passport.
What was in the bag? said
            the policeman.

Some money, a passport
            and a poem.

How did it go, that poem?

            I wish I could remember.

Anger filled her body and mind, it
permeated her insides, her throat
and heart throbbed with anger. ('Beware
the ire of the calm.') There was
anger in her teeth, nails and hair.
It drummed in her ears.
'How lovely to see you,' she said,
'Do sit down.'

The advantage of getting dim-sighted
is that there are only outlines and no dinkety details.
Everyone's skin is smooth.
Everyone's eyebrows are arches.
Everyone's eyes are black points.
Everyone's clothes are clean.
Telegraph poles look like poplars
And a dark room looks like it's supposed to be.
The pictures on the walls of the hotel
Look like art
And I can never find my glasses.

While Flicking Over the Pages

Noticed by chance an entry in
                     Who's Who
(b. 1912) the man so truly promising:
good school, Oxford, career in
                     Foreign Office,
Egypt, Greece, exotic places (but then
Paraguay—something of a comedown).
First novel well celebrated—remember,
they called him an artist to his
                     fingertips.
Now why, bewildered, does he
                     trot around,
an office-boy of literature, snatching
the opportunity to write a paragraph
of wasp-like criticism, here and there,
and tittle-tattle over the garden-fence?
Oh what went wrong and how
under the aspect of eternity
did his trivial genes develop, his fine ones
                     wither?

Standing in the Field

That scarecrow standing in the field
is dress-designed as if to move
all passers-by to tears
of sorrow for his turnip face,
his battered hat, his open arms
flapping in someone else's shirt,
his rigid, orthopedic sticks
astride in someone else's jeans,
one leg of which is short, one long.
He stands alone, he stands alone.

To the Gods of My Right Hand

Whoever the gods may be that come to occupy
the lodging of this limb, of them I make supplication
for the health of my right hand, waxing now
to her proper appointment; let them never forsake
her wrist's contrivances that strike at last
the waters of the Word where Babylon
enjoys no more her songs. Whoever the gods,
let them enter my right hand, never
to forget her cunning in the first and the last encounter.

That Lonely Shoe Lying on the Road

One sad shoe that someone has probably flung
out of a car or truck. Why only one?

This happens on an average one year
in four. But always throughout my
life, my travels, I see it like
a memorandum. Something I have
forgotten to remember,

　　　　that there are always
mysteries in life. That shoes
do not always go in pairs, any more
than we do. That one fits;
the other, not. That children can
thoughtlessly and in a merry fashion
chuck out someone's shoe, split up
someone's life.

　　　　But usually that shoe that I
see is a man's, old, worn, the sole
parted from the upper.
Then why did the owner keep the other,
keep it to himself? Was he
afraid (as I so often am with
inanimate objects) to hurt its feelings?

That one shoe in the road invokes
my awe and my sad pity.

The Victoria Falls

So hushed, so hot, the broad Zambesi lies
Above the Falls, and on her weedy isles
Swing antic monkeys swarm malignant flies,
And seeming-lazy lurk long crocodiles.
But somewhere down the river does the hush
Become a sibilance that hints a sigh,
A murmur, mounting as the currents rush
Faster, and while the murmur is a cry
The cry becomes a shout, the shout a thunder
Until the whole Zambesi waters pour
Into the earth's side, agitating under
Infinite spray mists, pounding the world's floor.
    Wrapped in this liquid turmoil who can say
    Which is the mighty echo, which the spray?

It occurs to me, perversely perhaps, but unmistakably,
That it would be so nice to be seized like that
And taken away.
Why?
I'm not sure why, but it occurs to me
That it would be so nice to have a change of problems,
And such a relief to be in the right for once
In the face of the interrogators which are everywhere, anyway.

Solitary confinement sounds nice, too.
I like that word, used in the reports, 'incommunicado'.
Why?
Well, why are you asking? I'm only just saying it occurs to me
That one might be able to take a spiritual
Retreat out of it, such as I've never managed
To achieve in the atmosphere of monasteries and convents.
Unworldliness is such a distraction, you see.

Of course, the idea of being seized is
A prehistoric female urge, probably, rising
Up from the Cave, which must have been exciting.
And perhaps one would hope for a charming interrogator.

Yes, I do agree, I wouldn't like it really.
It's only just an idea. Yes, I know you don't follow.
Because, in fact, I'm not leading anywhere. Only talking,
That's all. I think I'd put up a fight, actually,
If taken away off the street. And it occurs to me that maybe
I would like a fight, but not really.
Neither would they, perhaps.
Why?

I don't know. Why are you asking questions
Like this and trying to put me in the wrong?
I've exhausted the idea, anyhow, with all this talking.

Night, the wet, the onyx-faced
Over the street was shining where
I saw an object all displaced
In black water and black air.

Was it myself? If so I found
An odd capacity for vision.
Capacity, I understand
Is limited by fixed precision,

Being the measure of displacement:
The void exists as bulk defined it,
The cat subsiding down a basement
Leaves a catlessness behind it.

That vision then, shall I concede is
Proved by a void capacity?
What's good enough for Archimedes
Ought to be good enough for me.

But knowing little of natural law
I can't describe what happens after
You weigh a body such as I saw,
First in air and then in water.

Against the Transcendentalists

There are more visionaries
Than poets and less
Poets than missionaries,
Poets are a meagre species.

There is more vanity, more charity,
There is more of everything than poetry
Which, for personal purposes,
I wish may preserve
Identity from any other commodity
Also from Delphic insanity,
Drunkenness and discrepancy
Of which there's already a great plenty.
And so I reserve
The right not to try to
Fulfil the wilderness or fly to
Empyreal vacuity with an eye to
Publication, for what am I to
Byzantium or Byzantium
To me? I live in Kensington
And walk about, and work in Kensington
And do not foresee departing from Kensington.
So if there's no law in Kensington
Adaptable to verse without contravening
The letter to prove
The law, I'll make one.

The first text is
The word. The next is
(Since morals prevent quarrels
And writers make poor fighters)

Love your neighbour, meaning
Your neighbour, let him love
His neighbour, and he his.
Who is Everyman, what is he
That he should stand in lieu of
A poem? What is Truth true of?
And what good's a God's-eye-view of
Anyone to anyone
But God? In the Abstraction
Many angels make sweet moan
But never write a stanza down.
Poets are few and they are better
Equipped to love and animate the letter.

I therefore resign
The seven-league line
In footwear of super-cosmic design
To the global hops
Of wizards and wops;
Hoping that if Byzantium
Should appear in Kensington
The city will fit the size
Of the perimeter of my eyes
And of the span of my hand:
Hands and eyes that understand
This law of which the third
Text is the thing defined,
The flesh made word.

Shipton-under-Wychwood

Under Wychwood the growth and undergrowth
contend and do not mind how things exceptional
meander into landscape. They are drenched under
and under the repetitive green at last.
Fetched into chastity are fond extravagant
and noticeable doings and undertakings
whereover all the rhythms of Cotswold ride.

Ride, and have struck an ever-receding camp
over and over again, redundant time and tenses
disposing of themselves. What horses overtake them?
and what will become of the rare and royal hunters?
Prebend plunges over Plantagenet; it is all
over, then, with the legions of Rome before
finality, split-hooved, has taken over
Shipton under the forest, concealed in summer.

Two or three on the winter pavement talking,
One or two in the stubble field,
Idle, concerning miracles.

Voices are butter, but the eyes overtly
Detest another's dubious lips;
Eyes are blades where fancy breeds.

In boredom breeds, meanwhile remains to each
Enemy his friend, to every lying
Tongue an angel apiece.

The conversation therefore is in heaven,
Here on the streets of understanding
Here in the fields of bread.

When men are magic and air their advocates
Bide by the human grain and yet,
Though these offences needs must come,
Agree, sincere as light.

Blessed is the child of indiscretion talking,
And the orphan of indignation,
And before their Father's face, their conversations
Continually dancing.

Blessed are sons enticed to sea, and the mother
Constrained by wonder and by sign,
Their angels cover the face of the water,
And the water singeth a quiet tune.

Two or three must argue these contentions;
One or two in a winter season
Herein long since have plucked a sentiment or scandal.
But our conversation is in heaven.

The Card Party

Pacified, smooth as milk, by cakes and tea,
Four ladies took their chairs accordingly;
Each, picking up her cards in slow suspense,
Preened up her creamy neck to Providence.

Somewhat apart from this important four,
Two sisters, knitting, settled near the door,
Cautioned each other, bending eye to eye,
Then watched the game together in rivalry.

Each player felt reluctantly compelled
To know what mystery the other held;
As one white neck rose taller with desire
The other three stretched likewise snakier.

And all the afternoon, discomfited,
Those four swans turned disdainful head from head;
Erect, they cast their cards throughout the night.
Each throat thinned upwards like a stalagmite.

By dawn they bent and buried their flexible
Extending isthmuses beneath the table,
Upraising with apologetic pride
Those graceful members at the other side.

And what about the two beside the door?
They veered from cross to curious, hour by hour.
The knitting tangled, bound both necks askew,
And from this loggerhead a spiral grew

From which the sister-heads peered forth to pry—
What cards? All six coiled there, finally.
Set in a formal knot and inextricable,
Two died beside the door, four at the table.

How brave these darlings, and how marvellous
That all their lovely necks should mingle thus.
Thus twined it was in death they coincided
Who always in their lives had been divided.

Chrysalis

We found it on a bunch of grapes and put it
In cotton-wool, in a matchbox partly open,
In a room in London in winter-time, and in
A safe place, and then forgot it.

Early in the cold spring we said, 'See this!
Where on earth has the butterfly come from?'
It looked so unnatural whisking about the curtain:
Then we remembered the chrysalis.

There was the broken shell with what was once
The head askew; and what was once the worm
Was away out of the window, out of the warm,
Out of the scene of the small violence.

Not strange, that the pretty creature formalised
The virtue of its dark unconscious wait
For pincers of light to come and pick it out.
But it was a bad business, our being surprised.

Elegy in a Kensington Churchyard

Lady who lies beneath this stone,
Pupil of Time pragmatical,
Though in a lifetime's cultivation
You did not blossom, summer shall.

The fierce activity of grass
Assaults a century's constraint.
Vigour survives the vigorous,
Meek as you were, or proud as paint.

And bares its fist for insurrection
Clenched in the bud; lady who lies
Those leaves will spend in disaffection
Your fond estate and purposes.

Death's a contagion: spring's a bright
Green fit; the blight will overcome
The plague that overcame the blight
That laid this lady low and dumb,

And laid a parish on its back
So soon amazed, so long enticed
Into an earthy almanack,
And musters now the spring attack;
Which render passive, latent Christ.

This person never came to pass,
Being the momentary name I gave
To a slight stir in a fictitious grave
Wherein I found no form and face, alas,
Of Evelyn Cavallo, Evelyn of grass.

Therefore, therefore, Evelyn,
Why do you assert your so non-evident history
While all your feminine motives make a mystery
Which, to resolve, arise your masculine?
Why will you not lie down

At the back of the neither here not there
Where lightly I left you, Evelyn of guile?
But no, you recur in the orgulous noonday style,
Or else in your trite, your debonair
Postprandial despair.

The Rout

A battle between thousands of bees and wasps in the ancient church at Stockerton, near Market Harborough (Leics.) has ended in a victory for the wasps.

Since the battle started three weeks ago the church has been closed and no services have been held.

For years, the bees had been storing their honey under the roof. But the honey started to trickle down the walls. The smell attracted the wasps.

Thousands of bees have been killed and the wasps are now eating the honey.

It is hoped to reopen the church on Sunday.

(NEWS CHRONICLE, 7 September 1951)

From Oliver Cromwell's despatch to Speaker Lenthall dated 14 June 1645, from Market Harborough:

'This day we marched towards him. He drew out to meet us. Both armies engaged. We, after three hours fight very doubtful at last routed his army; killed and took about 5,000; very many officers, but of what quality we yet know not. We took also about 200 carriages, all he had, and all his guns, being twelve in number; whereof two were demi-culverins and (I think) the rest sakers . . . Sir, this is none other but the hand of God, and to him alone belongs the glory, wherein none are to share with him.'

I

'has ended in a victory for the wasps'
What's wasps?—
A species of bees, or bees
A sort of wasps? Look

Them up in the Pocket Book of
British Insects: The Honey Bee,
Not a native of Britain.
After escape from captivity,
Wild colonies in hollow trees

Or similar sites not uncommon,
But these are from domesticated stock.
Wasps: A common wasp colony in
August or September may contain
Many thousands but all of these
Except the queens
Die in the autumn.

II

'the honey started to trickle down the walls',
And that is sickening enough.
For years they stored the stuff under the roof
And summer had o'erbrimmed their clammy cells.
'And that is sickening enough', to use the phrase
Lawrence used about bees' ways;
('bees . . . cluster on their own queen.
And that is sickening enough.')
What Lawrence meant I mean,
Which is that humanity's
Different, or ought to be, from bees.
We who are of imported
Origin, wild or domesticated,
Are not so similar
To bees as wasps are,
But in smelling honey we
Are like enough to wasp and bee
To be what we ought not to be.

III

'The smell attracted the wasps.'
Thousands of upstarts out of paper cells
Form up, assault the established
Wax-works of the wealthy sweet with smells
From long-ago ancestral summers ravished.

Wasps that recently have been
Clustering on your own queen,
Witness the outcome:
The murder of innumerable bees,
'A victory for the wasps' 'but these
Die in the autumn.'

IV

To the Queen Wasp: a despatch from Buzzer Bummer
Dated nineteen-fifty-one, the end of summer,
From Stockerton church near Market Harborough:
    This day we marched towards her.
    She drew out to meet us. We,
    Since three weeks' fight at last routed her army.
    Took all stores. Killed many thousand.
    Madam, this is none other but the hand
Of God. 'The wasps are now eating the honey.'
'It is hoped to reopen the church on Sunday.'

Four People in a Neglected Garden

Not yet. That is the high concession,
Taking the best of it.
Dying, not dead, the neglected garden
Is passionate yet.

But we are a process no protracted
Parley with trowel and gravel will prolong.
Nature nurtured us too, and then neglected
To gauge how long the grass grew long.

We four are gardens and are guardians
Of gardens. No wonder we let the increase
Of grass grow under our feet and made our own
Seditious separate peace.

Because there is a truce before the tall tree bending
Falls in the end and withers,
Ourselves the occasion of afternoon's portending—
Lie, syringa; follow, rambler; stems, tumble together.

Like Africa

He is like Africa in whose
White flame the brilliant acres lie,
And all his nature's latitude
Gives measure of the simile.

His light, his stars, his hemisphere
Blaze like a tropic, and immense
The moon and leopard stride his blood
And mark in him their opulence.

In him the muffled drums of forests
Inform like dreams, and manifold
Lynx, eagle, thorn, effect about him
Their very night and emerald.

And like a river his Zambesi
Gathers the swell of seasons' rains,
The islands rocking on his breast,
The orchid open in his loins.

He is like Africa and even
The dangerous chances of his mind
Resemble the precipice whereover
Perpetual waterfalls descend.

We Were Not Expecting the Prince To-day

As stated above, we were not expecting . . .
All the same, you had better show him the sleeping
Beauty upstairs with her powder still intact,
While the whole court on sentry duty, believe it,
Propped in their wigs a century exact,
Deplore her blunder, or rather, misconceive it.

And you had better and better deliver
The bat from her tresses, dispose for a kiss
That bluff on her webby mouth, for suppose he should call it,
And give her a nudge, and she takes the hint, and this
Beauty be a cloud of powder over her pallet?

Communication

Seeing them in that semi-exclusive place
One would have thought the couple perfectly suited;
She with a spherical, he with a conical face;
He a tubular outline; she, fluted.

So it came as a surprise to the listener-in,
And later, to recall, a diversion,
To find them versed in symbols, but alas, tuning in
Each the wrong wavelength to a foreign station.

Take for instance his observation, 'I deplore
The present indiscriminate bankruptcy
Of flesh, time's daylight robbery.
I'm sure it has not been permitted before.'

Interrupted, however, by her statement, 'I
Shall try to get hold of seats for tomorrow and
See the robbers passing by:
A chance in a lifetime I understand.'

Created and Abandoned

Where have you gone, how has it ended with you,
people of my dreams, cut off in mid-life, gone to what grave?
It's all right for me. I'm fine. I always woke up when we parted
and saw it was only a dream. I took up my life
as I left it the day before. But you?—
like people with bound feet, or people not properly formed,
without further scope, handicapped. Sometimes I never knew
what you were going to say, didn't let you speak, but woke.
You being unreal after all, this means unwell. I worry about you.
Did something not happen to you after my waking?
Did something next not happen? Or are you
limbo'd there where I left you forever like characters
in a story one has started to write and set aside?

However bad-mannered you were, however amazing
in your style, I hope you're not looking for me
night after night, not waiting for me to come back.
I feel a definite responsibility for your welfare.
Are you all right?

The Goose

Do you want to know why I am alive today?
I will tell you.
Early on, during the food-shortage,
Some of us were miraculously presented
Each with a goose that laid a golden egg.
Myself, I killed the cackling thing and I ate it.
Alas, many and many of the other recipients
Died of gold-dust poisoning.

Sit in a chair.
Calm yourself in front of the fire
Because you have just arrived from a tour
Of No-Man's land.
No-Man took you by the hand.
No-Man showed you into a room
At the top of a tall emporium.
Nothing there
But a steel chair.
Nothing in it
But a filing cabinet.

And the steel chair said, 'How do you do
I sent for you.
Meet my Cabinet
I was just going to reshuffle it.'
And he opened a drawer and reshuffled it.
Then said, 'Bring in
The dancing girl.' All shimmering
Came she dancing, breasts bare,
She had electric in her hair
Which gave you a shock.
Each breast was an alarm clock.
One was set at ten to two,
The other at a quarter past,
And you couldn't say which of them was slow
Or which of them was fast.
'Meet this lady,' said the steel chair.
'Notice her lever movements, dear.
You know she is a social improvement
Newly devised,

The first resistance movement
To be officially recognised.
Necessary to the race
At any time in any place;
Observe her charming contours ticking round
Because the hour is at hand.'

'Which is the hour?' you certainly said,
'On the left or on the right?'
'Ah,' said the girl, 'I can't decide,
But the alarm's not set tonight.'

'That's all for now,' said the steel chair,
'Show the gentleman out, my dear.'

Bluebell Among the Sables

The visitor came clothed with sables,
My dark and social friend.
The afternoon prospered after its kind
But they bore me, those intimate parliaments,
Those tea-times wear my heart away.

So I took half my pleasure in the sables
That flowed across her arm, the chair, the floor,
Sleek and fathomless like contemplative,
Living animals, the deep elect,
In ceremonious most limp obedience.

But the dark skins did move, she felt them creep:
'My God! My sables!'
Indeed they were alive with a new life,
The sombre swiftly shot with quick and silver
Fur within fur. It was Bluebell, my beautiful,
My small and little cat pounding the sables.
Flat on her spine she tumbled them,
Shaking their kindly tails between her teeth.

'My furs! Your cat!' . . .
I said, 'No need for alarm;
Those dead pelts can't cause Bluebell any harm.'
Poor soul, this put her in the wrong;
As one who somehow fails the higher vision,
She was meek: 'They cost the earth, my furs.'
I stroked the comical creature, she the sables,
And all came even.

For she said there was no damage, no damage.
It may be she had profit of the event;
As for myself that moment was well spent
When I saw Bluebell pummelling the sables.
I have the image, the gratuitous image
Miserly seized: of sable wonders glowing,
An order of the profound earth, of roots
And minerals evolved in civil strands,
Defined in which, the sprite, like air and like
A dawn asperges, green-eyed Bluebell plying
The sensuous fabric with her shining pads.

There was some difficulty at first, hesitation
On the part of a nervous party who wanted to say
Something he couldn't recall; the Adult Education
Book had said it. that thing he wanted to say.

The managerial conference debate
Went on two hours like this until, slow
And tolerant, Piper got up to democrate,
With a university training behind him thirty years ago.

The face and form harmoniously convex.
He would, of course, say something statesmanlike,
Memorable. Piper was not sure
How to begin till a heavensent inspiration like
A splinter seemed to fly out of the floor:
'The human situation is becoming increasingly complex.'

In the car that night on the way to Sadler's Wells,
When he told his wife 'The human situation is
Becoming increasingly complex,' she thought her marriage
Well worth it, the way he put things in nutshells.

Canaan

She is committed to earth, and the earth
Is plighted forever to her.
The wilderness is prone to her.
The hopeful race of all the earth is
Betrothed to her, pleasant ground of expectation,
Lambent country of Canaan.

Jordan heaved his banks away.
Jordan's valley bubbled over
High between those opposites.
He rose by night; he dipped by day.
He dipped down for the hosts of the wilderness
And for the silver country of Canaan.

The men of the wilderness at Jordan's ford
Lifted the Ark of the Covenant on their shoulders.
Jordan fled for all his worth.
Jordan-bed lay smitten to dry boulders.
The wilderness bore the Ark of the Lord
Of all the earth
Into the holy country of Canaan.

Canaan's the land where the wilderness landed.
Therefore I am not altogether confounded
Still to discover a wilderness in her.
Jordan shed his ways, lifted up the river;
Canaan's husbanded
Now with a ploughing sword, she is anointed
With burning torrents, bridal country,
Canaan of loss.

There goes the leviathan in his glory;
But here dissembles that wilderness. Fowl and beast
Have no more wonderful identity.
The tribes of the pomegranates and the tribes of the yeast,
The families of rubies and the families of grass
Are one to another as waste and waste
In the arms of Canaan of silver dross.

But I am not altogether confounded
That so immanent and green and promised a land
Confounds me with seeming not what she seemed;
Seeing the hopeful race is covenanted
Not less to Canaan
Than Canaan to her promised wilderness,
Seeing default of the double covenant, seeing
Treachery to the warm harvest, no gathering in
Of the pearly vines of Canaan.
The same thing over and over again.
In this I am not altogether bewildered.

No year is twice the same, nor has occurred
Before. We bandy by the name of grief,
Grief which is like no other. Not a leaf
Repeats itself, we only repeat the word.
January, as usual, frigid. As before,
A silent stir in February. More
Of a stir in March. Activity
In April, as previously.
May, as usual, abundant. As before,
A superfluity in June. Greenery galore
Thereafter as always. The season exults.

But never the same reason warily
Secretes the same petal from the same
Pod of a single bud. The circumstances are

Everywhere novel. The results
Only appear similar.

Time lacks experience. Therefore I am not quite
Confounded by history,
Being of the hopeful race of the earth,
Promised to promise, a mystery to mystery,
By which I am not altogether mystified,
Since she is plighted to me, a wilderness, and I to
The silver country of Canaan.

The Nativity

I. THE CONVERSATION OF THE THREE WISE MEN

'Wind and slobber,' said the Flate, 'my words are
Slobber and wind whether I meet with another
Flate or no. I say there is no other.
And I say what only another Flate can gather.
Either way, what I say is air and water.'

The Droom said, 'You're a sly one:
I was given to understand you were a Droom.
Look at your lips hewn out of sallow amber.
Look at your funny head all amethyst-encrusted,
Cut square. I should have known there is
No other Droom on earth. No one's to be trusted.'

'I', said the Aspontal, 'began to realise
We could hope only to be useful to each other
That time we three were looking at maps and
Plotting the journey together. We had to devise
Some reason for coming, and started saying "brother"
To each other. Don't brother me please in future,
You with the square head and you with the eyes
Inside your ears, for I never really
Believed you were Aspontals. However,
We've got to follow the star.
We've got to be three.
We've got to be wise.
Till heaven and earth pass
One jot or one tittle shall in no wise pass.'

II. THE CONVERSATION OF THE SHEPHERDS

The Gladanka was saying, 'If a ewe gives
A dead lamb and you kick her three times thrice
In the face before sunset how many suns will
Rise before her blood stinks?' And the
Weezabaw laughed, rubbing his corns with a stone.
And the Shorket said, 'Sod the riddle the same as
You sodded the ewe.' The Gladanka was saying,
'I knew a ewe give a dead lamb every time
Till the farmer slit her belly and stuffed it back.'
And the Weezabaw laughed, 'Gladys,' he said,
'Gladys Barker was that ewe's name.' 'Sod the name,'
Said the Shorket, 'of the day I married hollow-
Bellied Gladys Barker. If she's a Shorket
I'm a cherub with six eyes.' The Gladanka was
Saying, 'Your teeth grow out of your chin, you
No-Gladanka.' And the Weezabaw laughed;
'You two,' said the Weezabaw, 'you two will be
The death of me. You ought to see yourselves.
Whatever you both are is far, far
Short of a Weezabaw. You with the vertical mouth,
Keep in your tongue or it will wash your ears; and
You with the nose on top of your head, smell out
The principalities of heaven for all of us.'

III. THE CONVERSATION AT THE INN

Samuel Cramer came down in the lift
And said, 'My bed's got bugs.
Where's the manager?'
And the girl at the desk replied, 'Not here.'

'Well find him quick,' said Samuel Cramer,
'My bed's got bugs.'
And the girl at the desk replied, 'What name please?'
'Samuel Cramer,' said Samuel Cramer.
'Not the poet!' said the girl at the desk.
'Well I used to be one,' said Samuel Cramer.
'How you've changed!' said the girl at the desk,
'You've done well for yourself, it's clear.'

'The manager, please,' said Samuel Cramer,
'I haven't a notion who you are.'
And the girl at the desk replied, 'He isn't here.
Don't you know La Fanfarlo the dancer?'

'You're the worse for the wear,' said Samuel Cramer,
'My bed's got bugs.'
And the Fanfarlo replied, 'I'll bump them flat for you
But no francs, please. We like dollars here.'

'Nothing doing,' said Samuel Cramer,
'Where's the manager?'
And the Fanfarlo replied, 'He's outside
Talking to a police inspector.'

'See, old soot,' said Samuel Cramer,
'I'm not here for your health.
I've come for a story for my paper.
What's going on round here?'

'The new tax,' said the Fanfarlo. 'We've got
A houseful of tax gatherers and tax payers;
And a man's wanted for murder, called Monteverde.
They think they've got him here. They say there's
Blood on his shirt and they were three days combing
The woods for him. A hot coming
He had of it I'm sure.'

'No good to me if it's local,'
Said Samuel Cramer.
'I thought there was going to be something big
According to a rumour.'

And the Fanfarlo replied, 'Clear out.'
'You anticipate me,' said Samuel Cramer.
'And pay before you go,' said the Fanfarlo.
'I'll see you in Hell,' said Samuel Cramer.

'I'll tell the manager,' yelled the Fanfarlo.
'Tell him,' said Samuel Cramer,
'That the bed's got bugs, the room reeks, and moreover
There's a mooing and bellowing going on
In the cattle shed beneath my window.
You'd think a cow was having a dozen
If it wasn't out of season.
But in this God-forsaken country anything could happen.'

IV. THE CONVERSATION OF THE ANGELS

Before the jubilees of Angels
    They said, 'What is that mess of meat and bone?'
Before the songs of Archangels
    They answered, 'That is no one.'

Before the concerts of Principalities
    They said, 'Who is no one?'
Before the dances of Virtues
    They answered, 'Man is no one,'

Before the lyres of Powers
    They said, 'Each man is one and Man is none.'

Before the voices of Dominations
    They said, 'Which man is like another?'
Before the clamours of Thrones
    They answered, 'None is like another man.'

Before the thunders of Cherubim
    They said, 'To whom is each man known?'
Before the swift motion of Seraphim
    They answered, 'Each is known to no man.'

An angel enquired of an Archangel, 'How many
Men have you seen?' And he replied, 'Plenty,
And women too. Divine affection
For them isn't easy. What a collection!'

A Virtue said to a Power, 'What ceases
When a man dies?' And he replied, 'A species,
Infinitely precious to God, being all
There is of his kind. He's irreplaceable.'

A Princedom asked of a Domination
'What is sin?' And he replied, 'The consumption
Of men by men. They've all got
An ache to eat what they are not.'

A Throne to a Cherub said,
'What do you reckon the price per head
Of men?' And he replied, 'I'm lost
Where sums are concerned. Ask the Holy Ghost.'

While the Seraphim got ready for the take-off—
    Six wings apiece, shot with bright shimmerings,
One said, 'What makes delight?'
    And one replied, 'The Queen of Heaven goes light.'
One said, 'What is to be made known?'
    And one replied, 'Men are to be made known.'

One said, 'What do these heavy six wings signify?'
   And one replied, 'Two to cover the face, two to
      cover the feet, and two to fly.'
One said, 'What do these dances signify?'
   And one replied, 'The resolution of discrepancy.'
One said, 'Fly, fly, for the love
   Of discrepancy most common.'
And one replied, 'Fly, fly,
   For the resolution of
   Common incongruity.'
One said, 'What's common to men?'
   And one replied, 'Uncommonness alone.
   Fly, for the grace
   Of common uncommonness
   Which is to be made known.
   Uncommon men become
   Common to men in Christ's face,
   Mediator of angels and of men.'

The Three Kings

Where do we go from here?
We left our country,
Bore gifts,
Followed a star.
We were questioned.
We answered.
We reached our objective.
We enjoyed the trip.
Then we came back by a different way.
And now the people are demonstrating in the streets.
They say they don't need the Kings any more.
They did very well in our absence.
Everything was all right without us.
They are out on the streets with placards:
Wise Men? What's wise about them?
There are plenty of Wise Men,
And who needs them?—and so on.

Perhaps they will be better off without us,
But where do we go from here?

Sisera, dead by hammer and nail, fared worst
Where he fared well; the women had fed him first.
After the kill Deborah came,
A holy kite to claim the heathen viscera.
Is not her song impressive? All the same,
I am for Sisera

Whose ruin had rhetoric enough and fitness
For Deborah's prophecy, so are God's enemies supplanted.
She needed no polemic, as God was her witness
Gloriously to publish the story condensed:
'The stars in their courses fought against
Sisera,' she descanted.

The hostess it was, who pinned the villain mute;
But Deborah whittled her fine art, the keener to spike him
On a final point: 'His women wait for the loot.'
So, from God's poets may God perfectly defend
Sisera and all the rest of us like him,
With whom the stars contend.

The Ballad of the Fanfarlo

Samuel Cramer, qui signa autrefois du nom de Manuela de Monteverde quelques folies romantiques, — dans le bon temps du Romantisme, — est le produit contradictoire d'un blême Allemand et d'une brune Chilienne.

BAUDELAIRE

I

Samuel Cramer came down in the lift,
Walked into the street and shut the door.
Behind him lay a settlement of fever,
The tremorous metropolis, before.

The first crossing that Samuel Cramer came to
A green light showed up and spoke to him,
'I see you are a man with fever on you
In the middle year of your time.'

The second crossing that Samuel came to
He stood beneath the yellow rays:
'I fear you are a man alarmed with fever
In the middle year of your days.'

The third crossing that he came to
He saw a red light there,
And the light said, 'Halt, you feverish traffic
And tell me what you are.

'Now tell, now tell, your title and kind,
And tell, you feverish fellow
That wander this metropolis
From the green light to the yellow.'

'Oh I am Samuel Cramer,' he said,
'Born of a German father
Who was as pale as my naked bone,
And a brown Chilean mother.'

'And where do you come from, Samuel Cramer,
From the yellow light to the red?'
'I come from the dancing Fanfarlo.
She lies on her fever bed.'

'And where are you going, Cramer,
In the middle year of your time?'
'I go to seek my true friend,
Manuela de Monteverde his name.

'I wander this metropolis
In the good year of my prime.
By all the lights that are in the sun
I fevered go to claim
Manuela de Monteverde
Who is my heart's fame.

'The breath of my infection,
The water of my name,
Float in the null subtraction
That parted me from him,
Manuela de Monteverde
Who is my heart's fame.'

'Follow me, follow me, now Samuel Cramer,
My dear master to see
That sits in this metropolis,
For I think you lie to me.'

Samuel Cramer turned his footsteps.
The green light and the yellow said no word;

And he had come to a high hostel
With the red light for his guard.

Samuel Cramer went up in the lift,
Walked into a room and shut the door.
Behind him lay the streets of the tremorous city,
A steel desk and a chair, before.

'And what are you,' said the steel chair.
'With my little red light for a guard,
That come through the quivering streets of the city,
Where the green light and the yellow say no word?'

'My name is Samuel Cramer,' he said,
'Born of a Chilean mother
Who was as brown as my bone's marrow,
And a white German father.'

'Now if you are,' said the steel chair,
'Of a Chilean mother brown
And a white father from Germany,
Then you are No Man.

'And where do you come from, Samuel Cramer,
From the green light to the red?'
'I come from the dancing Fanfarlo
Laid out on her fever bed.'

'I think you lie, false Samuel Cramer,
Two times you lie,' the steel chair said,
'For a hundred years have come and gone
And the Fanfarlo lies dead.

'And where are you going, Samuel Cramer,
In the middle year of your days?'
'I seek Manuela de Monteverde
Who is my heart's praise.

94

'And all my nights of fever
And all my shifting days
Are an infernal river
Between my sight and his,
Manuela de Monteverde
Who is my heart's praise.'

'You lie, you lie, false Samuel Cramer,
Three times you lie as you stand there,
For Manuela de Monteverde
He is a steel chair.

'Now follow, now follow, Samuel Cramer,
Now follow my little red guard
To No-Man's sanatorium
In the antiseptic ward.

'And they shall rip you breast from back
And ask your white bone
If you are born of German father
And a Chilean mother brown.

'They shall rip you lung and lights
And ask of your brown marrow
If you are come from the fever bed
Of the dancing Fanfarlo.

'And they shall rip you throat to thigh
And ask your false heart
If Manuela de Monteverde
Was ever of that part.'

Samuel Cramer went down in the lift,
Walked through the tremorous streets with the little guard,
And he had come to No-Man's sanatorium
In the antiseptic ward.

'Now bless this day,' cried Samuel Cramer,
'That I have lived to win.
It is not for my white father
Nor for my mother brown,
It is not for the Fanfarlo
That the fever has put down,
But Manuela de Monteverde,
For his sake I'll suffer pain.'

Then up and said an ether-bowl,
'You bless this day too fine,
For in the antiseptic ward
I think you will feel no pain.'

'Then praise this day,' cried Samuel Cramer,
'That I have lived to see.
It is not for my Chilean mother
Nor for my father from Germany,
It is not for the Fanfarlo
That the fever has laid by,
But Manuela de Monteverde,
For his sake I'll die.'

Then up and spoke a little keen knife,
'You praise this day too high,
For in this sanatorium
I think you will not die.'

Samuel Cramer laid his head down,
And he was locked in an anaesthetic sleep.
The ether-bowl stood over him
And the keen knife ripped him up.

And first they found his white bone,
And next his brown marrow,
And when they found his feverish heart
They said, 'He is No Man that we know.

'If he is the son of a German father
And a Chilean mother brown,
Speak the word, you white bone.'
But answer they got none.

'If he is come from the Fanfarlo
That the fever has put down,
Speak the word, you brown marrow.'
But answer they got none.

'If Manuela de Monteverde
Was ever his benison,
Speak the word, you feverish heart.'
Answer they got none.

Then up and rose the little red light,
And he had run through the long streets of the city.
'Now hear, now hear, my master dear,
The news of my day's duty.

'Oh, they have asked his brown marrow
And they asked his white bone,
And they asked his false heart also,
But answer they got none.'

'He lied, he lied,' the steel chair said,
'Three times he lied as he stood here,
For a white father and a brown mother
Can never a man bear;
The dancing Fanfarlo is married
And buried a hundred years or more;
And Manuela de Monteverde
He is a steel chair.'

II

The noise of a fog-horn out behind the window,
As well as the smell of gas,
And visible air of a metropolitan yellow,
And also the taste of withered cress,
And the chill of a zinc pillow:
All were assembled, having come concerning
Samuel Cramer, who woke before the morning.

'Whatever's in my nostril is an element
No different from the mist I cannot see through,
And the same as a mouthful of sour condiment,
As it might be a cold white slab for my pillow.
In all I hear the siren vigilant:
Far away the fog must be on the river,
But where am I?' cried Samuel Cramer.

'The cloud, the taste, the smell, are feverish fancies;
The touch and the sound are past all reasoning;
For now I see a row of slender benches,
On each a narrow sleeper lying,
And every sleeper bound with bandages:
They must be in a hellish dormitory,'
Cried Samuel Cramer, 'but where am I?'

'Oh, where am I, you slender sleepers?'
Then the four walls answered him,
'You lie in the convalescent ward
Of No-Man's sanatorium.'

A bell rang and the day came in
And every sleeper woke,
Peered through a slit in his bandages
As the four walls spoke.

Samuel Cramer looked at his own full length,
Saw that his long length was bandaged whole,
And he looked again at the narrow benches
And said, 'Who are you all?'

'Who are you all?' cried Samuel Cramer,
'And what were the ailments
That brought you to lie in this dormitory
All bound in hellish cerements?'

'I am No Man,' said one, 'but I was a miller.
For several centuries I stood and ground
The daily grind, and was getting tired of it
Just when I met with my true friend.

Who being a miller of high ability
Turned the course of a whole river
To turn my mill, and still in my dreams I glorify
Manuela de Monteverde and enjoy him forever.'

'I was a soldier,' said another; 'now I am No Man;
Served in all the big wars in every land
From Gaul to Brazil. Was working my ticket
Just when I met up with my true friend.
Now he was a soldier could take on an army
With catapult, cutlass or cartridge, and never
Came but he killed, and still I glorify
Manuela de Monteverde and enjoy him forever.'

'I was a scholar,' another said, 'early Dispontium
Was my special department, and I had come to the end,
As I had thought, of research on Dispontine manners
Just when I met my true and learned friend,
Who pointed out a significant point when he
In course of research was of course the first to discover

The Dispontii ate cross-legged, therefore I glorify
Manuela de Monteverde and enjoy him forever.'

'I was one,' said the next, 'who gathered impressions,
And now I am No Man, but there was a day
When I sat on the steps of cultural buildings
And watched the people passing by;
So bored, I almost would have done something about it.
But another sat beside me, and silent together
We communed with each other, so I glorify
Manuela de Monteverde and enjoy him forever.'

'I knew the Industry inside-out
And now am No Man,' said another,
'But still I remember things were tight
Until I took up with a business partner.
He was a brilliant man, definitely.
Take his sales record. Look at the clever
Way he shoved those shares around. I glorify
Manuela de Monteverde and enjoy him forever.'

'Now one and all,' cried Samuel Cramer,
'In Manuela de Monteverde's name
I say he is a feverish poet
In the middle year of his time.'

Then each one cried, 'You false witness,'
And each sat up to testify
In Manuela de Monteverde's name,
And each one said, 'You lie.'

'You lie, you lie,' cried each to each,
And each to each arose,
And they had fallen all on all
And felled them with bitter blows.

They ripped them bandages from bone,
They ripped them bone and hair:
They were not done till everyone
Lay level in a smear.

The bones lay loose on the white zinc floor
In Manuela de Monteverde's name,
All in the convalescent ward
Of No-Man's sanatorium.

All in the convalescent ward
Of No-Man's sanatorium
A bell rang and the night came in
And settled over them.

'Now praise this night,' cried each to each,
'For I lie so bloodily
In Manuela de Monteverde's name,
And surely I shall die.'

Samuel Cramer lay on his loose bones,
Stared out of the window where there was
The new moon like a pair of surgical forceps
With the old moon in her jaws.

And in there came a bandage-roll
And a bottle of germicide,
And they had bound the loose bones
On the narrow benches laid.

The second day, a bell rang;
Then each to each called out,
'I fear that there's no dying here
But I shall rip your throat.'

And filament from ligament were parted
When in there came a roll of bandages
And a little bottle of disinfectant
To bind them up on narrow benches.

And the third day they turned again,
And they had hacked them bone from bone.
'I see three ghosts,' cried Samuel Cramer then,
'They do not come too soon.'

'I see three ghosts,' cried Samuel Cramer,
'And they have come too slow.
The one is Manuela de Monteverde.
The next is the Fanfarlo.
The third is a fiend that hovers behind,
And he is no man that I know.'

Then in there came a bottle of germicide
With a roll of bandages,
All in the convalescent ward
To bind them up regardless.

III

There was a sound of breathlessness by dawn;
Asthmatical, it changed into a yawn,
And Manuela de Monteverde bore
His bulky vapour up against the door.

Excogitated, it was tiresome
Being the fattest ghost in Christendom;
Looked at the narrow benches with regret,
Shuffled and lit a stubble cigarette.

And underneath an airy domino
Rattled the members of the Fanfarlo,
The ancient vertebrae inflexible
Still she contrived a clamorous *pas seul*;

Scattered her jewels in their sockets loose
That fell about her height in bright disuse.
All up and down the convalescent ward
Came she a fabulous camelopard.

And there was another that hovered behind.
It was a fog that might have been a fiend
Or an angel caught in a cataleptic pause
For all it looked like anything that is.

And silent, with ambiguous intent,
This hovered in its own environment.
The air of No-Man's sanatorium
Seemed epileptic by comparison.

Samuel Cramer rose from his narrow bed.
'Now praise this day at last,' he cried.
'I see Manuela de Monteverde plain
Though he is fat that once was lean.

'I see you plain, my true friend
Who come so tardily.
In No-Man's sanatorium
For your sake I lie.

'And daily, daily, for your sake
I suffer my heart's bane
Which is destruction without death,
Destruction with no pain.

'And whether you were a false friend
Or whether you were a true,
Deliver me now from this limbo
    And I shall follow you.

'And I shall follow you night and day
In the world invisible,
And were you a false friend or a true,
I'll follow in Heaven or in Hell.'

Manuela de Monteverde spread
His open palms, sunk in the spongy wrists.
'Speaking as a ghost,' he said, 'I am a man
For whom the visible world exists.

'And if you should follow, my dear fellow,
No Heaven and no Hell would you see,
Nor love nor hate where I stagnate
In a limbo of sympathy.

'True, I was a false friend but first I was a true,
And I went to the grave, but never could forget
How all of you have magnified my name;
I have grown fat on that magnificat.

'And now am stuck in a deadlock of affection,
And I suppose, so long as I remember
The glory of man each man will glorify
Man and destroy him forever.

'So if you must follow, my dear fellow,
I think you should follow not me,
For I swear it's neither here nor there
In a limbo of sympathy.'

'Oh I must part from you,' said Samuel Cramer,
'And you must part from me,
But Manuela de Monteverde
My heart's fame will ever be.

'And I shall smite the light of the sun
And harrow the earth's face,
And I'll contend until I find
A way to depart in peace.'

All in the convalescent ward,
A bony ghost was rattling to and fro.
'I see my long, long, love,' cried Samuel Cramer,
'And she is the dancing Fanfarlo.

'I see you plain, my long, long, love,
And gawky is your tread,
And you have gone to skin and bone
Since you lay on the fever bed.

'Now whether you were a false love,
Or whether you were a true;
Take me away from my misery
And I shall follow you.

'And I shall follow you day and night
In the world invisible,
And were you a false love or a true
I'll dance with you in Heaven or in Hell.'

'I can't stop now,' said the Fanfarlo,
'Although I'm short of breath,
For I'm employed on the skeleton staff
Of the dancing troupe of Death.'

She passed him by, and her step was high,
Over her shoulder calling shrill,
'After I lay on the fever bed
I rose and married well.

'I tired of that, and went to the grave,
But I could not forget
My macabaresque that was such a success
And my famous pirouette,

'Till Death, the talent-scout, took me up,
And now he hovers at my back
Like a fiend that looks like nothing on earth,
And I think that my bones will break.

'So if you would follow, my sweet fellow,
Be sure it's your vocation,
For there's no peace being caught like this
In a limbo of agitation.'

'Then you must part from me,' cried Samuel Cramer,
'And I must part from you,
But in Heaven or in Hell I shall remember
The dancing Fanfarlo.

'And I shall shift the files of the stars
Until the empyreal orders cease,
And I'll confound until I find
A way to depart in peace.'

All in the convalescent ward
A silent fog was hovering,
And it might have been leviathan
For all it looked like anything.

'Now Death I see you plain,' said Samuel Cramer,
'Oh you have come too slow.
Come out like a man and reason with me
For I would reason with you.

'For I am Samuel Cramer,' he said,
'And I am the natural meridian
Of a father and mother, north and south,
And am I not a man?

'Excellently I was virtuous
And viciously I sinned,
Slowly, slowly, lost my looks
Alas, and I'd read all the books
Before I came to No-Man's sanatorium
Where death is in my mind.'
Then Death spoke courteously to Samuel Cramer,
And Death said, 'Are you blind?'

'I am not blind,' said Samuel Cramer,
'And all things low and great,
That I have seen beneath the sun
I never shall forget.

'For I have seen the bright things and the black,
And I have seen enough
To make me as fit a man for Heaven
As I am for Hell, in my belief.'
Then Death spoke courteously to Samuel Cramer,
And Death said, 'Are you deaf?'

'I am not deaf,' said Cramer,
'And I have listened day and night,
And every word that I have heard
I never shall forget.

'For I have heard the innocent voice
And I have heard the foul,
And I am as fit a man for Heaven
As I am fit for Hell.'
Then Death spoke courteously to Samuel Cramer,
And Death said, 'Can you feel?'

'Oh I can feel!' cried Samuel Cramer,
'For I have fondled cold and heat.
There's no transaction in all sensation
But I have had to do with it.

'For I have drunk the subtle water
And eaten ruinous bane,
And I have smelt the melancholy vapour,
As well as the stanchless fume of carrion.
Each device of sin and grace
Has made me and undone.

'Now I am fit to be let beyond the sheer
Celestial pale, and driven
Before the glaciers that ride
All the precipitous streets of Heaven.

'And I am able to handle infernal cosmetics
And blacken my arms like vile
Branches that hoe the storm-sky,
Feverish culture of Hell.

'So I shall follow you night and day
In the world invisible,
And speak the fame for all I have done
To Heaven or to Hell.'

Then Death spoke courtesously to Samuel Cramer,
And Death said, 'I admire your memory

And also the fame of all you have done,
Likewise your marvellous delivery.

'And for all you are gagged and riven here
You have my sympathy.
Now the fittest place for such a case
Is surely a limbo of memory.'

'But I'll not go to a limbo,' cried Samuel Cramer,
'And I have been gagged and riven
For nothing less than to go in peace
To Hell or to Heaven.'

Then Death said, 'Heaven is not my province
And Hell is not my territory,
So if you must follow, my true fellow,
I think you should follow not me.'

'But I shall follow you,' said Samuel Cramer,
'To the world invisible
Where I'll be free to hack my way
To the bounds of Heaven or Hell.

'Oh I shall rock the ethereal foundations,
Wherever the world invisible is,
And I shall rend until I find
A way to depart in peace.'

'The terms of departure in the peace treaty,'
Said Death,
'According to our annals,
Provide for a proper mortality
Only through the proper channels.

'And according to the formula
That I am furnished with,

There is a staple amnesia
That leeches to the pith.

'It's blind, it's blind, the keen-eyed kind,
It's deaf, the sedulous ear,
And words of legendary address
Swallow each other's pointedness
In the place where I transpire.

'This is the formula that moles
Its blind way to Heaven or Hell;
And sometimes in the last event
I hear a solitary call:
Sever my ears in a hundred years
But let me listen a while.

'And often I hear a lonely noise
Before the dark sets in:
Make me null at a distant spell
But leave me rife till then.
And mortified from every side
The voice of memory comes crying.

'It's *Hey, Death!* and it's *Hoa, Death!*
Will you remember me?
But there's no clause for a personal case
Laid down in the peace treaty.

'It's checked, it's checked, the retrospect,
It's lapsed, the sympathetic kind,
And agitation's under stress
Of a rigid absent-mindedness
In the place where I impend.

'So if you must follow, my true fellow,
I think you should follow not me,

For there's no scope for a talented type
In the loss of memory.'

All in the convalescent ward,
A bell rang, and the night came in,
And every man an enemy
On the narrow benches lying.

'I call you all,' cried Samuel Cramer,
'To witness my treachery
If I contact the false pact
That was offered me this day.

'And when the hawk shall creep in the earth
And hogs nest in the sun,
Then I'll forget the prime estate
Of all things I have known.

'When the lizard mates with Pegasus
And the lynx lies with the roe,
Then I'll forget the black and the bright
The high delight and the low,
Manuela de Monteverde
And the dancing Fanfarlo.'

FROM THE LATIN

Persicos odi, puer, apparatus:
Displicent nexae philyra coronae:
Mitte sectari, rosa quo locorum
 Sera moretur.
Simplici myrto nihil allabores
Sedulus curo: neque te ministrum
Dedecet myrtus, neque me sub arta
 Vite bibentem.

Persicos Odi

(*Horace I, xxxviii,*
in the Jacobean mode)

Weave in my garland, boy, no more
The trash of Persia, and dispose
Therein not linden nor the rare
    Protracted rose.

Thus plainly twine the myrtle wreath
Which well accords thy servient mien,
And well thy master, drinking 'neath
    The trellised vine.

Solvitur acris hiems grata vice veris et Favoni:
  Trahuntque siccas machinae carinas.
Ac neque jam stabulis gaudet pecus, aut arator igni;
  Nec prata canis albicant pruinis.
Jam Cytherea choros ducit Venus, imminente Luna:
  Junctaeque Nymphis Gratiae decentes
Alterno terram quatiunt pede; dum gravis Cyclopum
  Volcanus ardens visit officinas.
Nunc decet aut viridi nitidum caput inpedire myrto,
  Aut flore, terrae quem ferunt solutae.

To Lucius Sestius in the Spring

(from Horace I, iv)

A change in the weather. Winter's edge breaks to the
    soft west wind.
  Now they are rolling the dry keels down to the sea;
And the cattle no longer huddle in the stalls, nor the
    ploughman over his fire,
  Nor the fields blench frozen under a film of rime.

But Cythera (call her Venus if you like) is leading the
    dance now,
  By the light of the pendulous moon, her girls are
    linking
Delectable arms and shaking the earth with their feet,
    keeping time;
  Ferocious Vulcan's away meanwhile, inspecting his
    armaments factory.

Now's the time to dress yourself up: bind your brows
    with myrtle
  Or with your pick of the earth's yield; it's offered
    unstintingly;
Now is the time to sacrifice a lamb to the faun in the
    shadows
  Of the sacred wood—or give him a kid if he prefers
    it.

Nunc et in umbrosis Fauno decet immolare lucis,
    Seu poscat agna, sive malit haedo.
Pallida mors aequo pulsat pede pauperum tabernas,
    Regumque turris. O beate Sesti,
Vitae summa brevis spem nos vetat inchoare longam.
    Jam te premet nox, fabulaeque Manes,
Et domus exilis Plutonia: quo simul mearis,
    Nec regna vini sortiere talis;
Nec tenerum Lycidan mirabere, quo calet juventus
    Nunc omnis, et mox virgines tepebunt.

Know, Sestius, my lucky one, that pale impartial
      death will knock as hard
   At the gates of a royal fortress as he will at a small
      hut door.
Remember, there's only a lifetime to measure hope by,
   And night's got you marked already; old legendary
         ghosts move inward,

And not far below, there's a household of shades: once
      there,
         you'll never more
   Throw the dice for the odds of being wine-host,
Nor marvel at exquisite Lycidas who infatuates all the
      boys,
   Though the girls will soon begin to warm to him
      too.

Vides, ut alta stet nive candidum
    Soracte, nec jam sustineant onus
  Silvae laborantes, geluque
    Flumina constiterint acuto.
Dissolve frigus, ligna super foco
Large reponens; atque benignius
  Deprome quadrimum Sabina,
    O Thaliarche, merum diota.
Permitte Divis caetera: qui simul
Stravere ventos aequore fervido
  Deproeliantis, nec cupressi,
    Nec veteres agitantur orni.
Quid sit futurum cras, fuge quaerere; et
Quem fors dierum cumque dabit, lucro
  Appone: nec dulcis amores
    Sperne puer, neque tu choreas.
Donec virenti canities abest
Morosa; nunc et campus, et areae,
  Lenesque sub noctem susurri
    Composita repetantur hora:
Nunc et latentis proditor intimo
Gratus puellae risus ab angulo,
  Pignusque dereptum lacertis,
    Aut digito male pertinaci.

Winter Poem

(from Horace I, ix)

Look up at Mount Soracte's dazzling snow
Piling along the branches that can barely
   Withstand its weight, while piercing ice
     Impedes the river's flowing!

So, Thaliarch, let's dissolve the cold, stacking
The hearth with logs, and with a rash indulgence
   Fetch up the four-year vintage jars
     Of undiluted Sabine wine.

The rest leave to the gods at whose command
Contending winds and seething seas desist
   Until the sacred cypress-tree
     And ancient ash no longer quake.

Then cast aside this contemplation of
The future. Better reckon the random day's
   Advantage, child, and don't despise
     Parties and love and those sweet things.

While boyhood still forestalls cantankerous age,
Now is the time appropriate to whispered
   Seductive twilight messages
     In city courts and empty lots.

And now's your time for secret pleasantries
With a girl-friend mocking from her corner ambush—
   The time to steal a token from
     Her arm, or half-protesting finger.

Vivamus, mea Lesbia, atque amemus,
Rumoresque senum severiorum
Omnes unius aestimemus assis.
Soles occidere, et redire possunt:
Nobis, quum semel occidit brevis lux,
Nox est perpetua una dormienda.
Da mi basia mille, deinde centum,
Dein mille altera, dein secunda centum,
Deinde usque altera mille, deinde centum,
Dein quum millia multa secerimus,
Conturbabimus illa, ne sciamus,
Aut ne quis malus invidere possit,
Quum tantum sciat esse basiorum.

Prologue and Epilogue

(after Catullus)

PROLOGUE

(Nox est perpetua una dormienda)

Let's live Catullus, or else let us love—
One or the other, though rumour now
Lets live and love till the sun goes out.
The daylight lasts too long for us
Who follow after our wills' distortion
Along forevers of chosen darkness.

Those lovers were simple as fire but we
Advance into ice; they melted like rivers
But we are others; pale northman,
Resist that sun that shall offend you;
Be dumb, though time upon time I call
Catulle to the ancient stones or sing
These epithalamia always arrested.

Furi et Aureli, comites Catulli:
Sive in extremos penetrabit Indos,
Litus ut longe resonante Eoa
    Tunditur unda:
Sive in Hircanos, Arabasque molles,
Seu Sacas, sagittiferosque Parthos,
Sive qua septemgeminus colorat
    Aequora Nilus:
Sive trans altas gradietur Alpes,
Caesaris visens monumenta magni
Gallicum Rhenum, horribilesque, ulti-
    mosque Britannos:
Omnia haec, quaecunque feret voluntas
Caelitum, tentare simul parati,
Pauca nuntiate meae puellae
    Non bona dicta;
Cum suis vivat, valeatque moechis,
Quos simul complexa tenet trecentos,
Nullum amans vere, sed idemtidem omnium
    Ilia rumpens.
Nec meum respectet, ut ante, amorem;
Qui illius culpa cecidit, velut prati
Ultimi flos, praetereunte postquam
    Tactus aratro est.

EPILOGUE

(Furi et Aureli, comites Catulli)

You, Hate and Love, companions of this poet
Where cities of fire sustain me, and where
The glaciers clash together the northern tundras'
    Assaulted waters,

Shall face these weathers of my instruction.
Then travel courageously, notorious couriers
Into the icelock, and beyond its zero
    Seek out my love.

Remind him first of all how he survives
The flower of death blown over that relinquished
Meadow where lover and plough break
    Lover and flower alike.

But let him not believe that a winter invoked
Can blight the bespoken summers nor silence him
Being that one who called time upon time,
    Lesbia to the ancient stones.

Index of Titles And First Lines